Sarah,

Psalm of My Heart:

Who We Are In Christ

Your purpose in life is found In Christ

Rebekah Lea Phelps

Rebekah Lea Phelps

Cover design by Teddi Black
www.teddiblack.com

First published by Dog Ear Publishing
4011 Vincennes Rd
Indianapolis, IN 46268
www.dogearpublishing.net

ISBN: 978-1-4575-3935-0

This book is printed on acid-free paper.

Printed in the United States of America

Table of Contents

My gratitude goes to

God my Father,

God my Savior,

and God the Holy Spirit.

Without You, I'm nothing.

I love you so much,
the Author and Finisher of my Story,

[signature]

Psalm of my Heart

Father, I just wanted to thank you that because of your love, I am....

Your child, born again of the *incorruptible seed, of* **THE WORD of GOD,** *which lives and abides forever.* Thank you for forgiving me of all my sins and washing me in the oh-so precious blood of your son, **JESUS CHRIST!** Your **HOLY SPIRIT** drew me and caused me to cry out, and you heard and made haste to respond to me! You have made me into a *new creature,* you took away my *heart of stone* and replaced it with a *heart of flesh,* and my body is the temple of the **HOLY SPIRIT,** where he resides. Your joy is my strength.

You have delivered me from the power of darkness and brought me into the Kingdom, your Kingdom, of marvelous light! Redeeming me from the curse of the law, bestowing abundant grace upon me, where sin abounds. I am blessed and a saint. You have set an angel to watch over me to keep me from dashing my foot against a stone. My heel crushes the head of the serpent because you gave me the authority to do so, and made me the head and not the tail. I'm above and not beneath. I am Holy as you are **HOLY** and without blame before you in love elect, established to the end. Justified, sanctified and set apart by you. Before I was born, you knew me in my mother's womb and consecrated me unto yourself.

I have been drawn near to you, by you, and made victorious by the **BLOOD OF CHRIST.** I am set free and made strong in my weaknesses, rich not poor, more than a conqueror, and a joint heir with **CHRIST**. It is because of your son that I can become complete, sealed with the **HOLY SPIRIT,** and accepted in **THE BELOVED**. It was him who was crucified, and my sin with him, so it is no longer I who live, but **CHRIST** lives in me. Standing free from condemnation, reconciled to you **GOD**, and qualified to share in the inheritances **THE WORD** speaks of. It speaks of them to the chosen, elect and firstborns, which I am. You have turned my mourning into joy. You have restored my soul.

Father, because I am firmly rooted, built up and established in my faith, I am overflowing with gratitude! You circumcised me with the circumcision made without hands, and to think me, "The Chief of all Sinners," has been made a fellow citizen with the saints of your household! Built upon the foundation of the Apostles and Prophets, **JESUS CHRIST**, himself, being the **CHIEF CORNER STONE**. Yes, to think...I was born of you **GOD**, and the evil one does not touch me, because I abide under the shadow of the Almighty. You are my fortress and my refuge and as you cover me, I am rising UP with wings as an eagle! To know I am the righteousness of **GOD**, in **CHRIST JESUS**, and am a partaker of his divine nature! Yes, I have the mind of **CHRIST**.

Everything my hand touches, you cause it to prosper. I've been granted *favor* with you and with man. I have received power, the power of the **HOLY SPIRIT**, to *lay hands on the sick, to recover sight to the blind* (in the natural and the spiritual), *power to cast out demons; power over all the power of the enemy* and *nothing shall by any means hurt me.* I have been anointed to *set captives free, heal the broken hearted,* and *signs and wonders will follow me* as I continue to believe and follow you, as your disciple. Teaching as you teach me, interceding with you for who you will, as **THE GREAT INTERCESSOR**, sitting at the right hand of your throne, intercedes on and for my behalf.

You are my Shepherd, you have lead me beside still waters, to rest, to drink, to cry and to laugh. Yes, there is a time for everything. Thank you Lord for being my **FAITH-FUL FRIEND**.

You set me here upon earth, for a time and a season, *to be* the light of the world and the salt of the earth. Your representative, a living epistle, an ambassador called and chosen. Praise you **FATHER** for giving me **LOVE** for the human race, because without **LOVE**, I would have nothing. I have not been given the spirit of fear (which is contrary to Love) but of power, love and a sound mind, whereby I cry; **ABBA FATHER**! Yes, the apple of my **FATHER'S** eye. Whom I have dove's eyes for. I am his bride and HE is my husband, **HIS NAME IS THE LORD OF HOST**.

I am healed by the stripes of **JESUS**. No plague shall come near my dwelling and any weapon that is formed against me shall not prosper! I am being changed into His image, raised up and one with **CHRIST** and seated in Heavenly Places. I am beloved by you **GOD**. I thank you that I have access by one **SPIRIT** unto you, the **FATHER**, and I overcome the world, because **CHRIST** was an overcomer and **THE WORD** says *greater* works will I do. Thank you for the ever-lasting life I have and the **GLORY** *of the* **LORD** that has *risen* upon me. Thank you for taking away the shame of my youth, I am not condemned and stand free of guilt. There is never a reason for me to hide anything from you or man because my life is hid with **CHRIST** in you **GOD**. **THE PEACE** of **GOD** which passes all understanding is mine and I possess it. I will lay down my life for others as your son lovingly laid his down for me. Besides, if I sought to save it…I would lose it. Thank you **FATHER** that you think good thoughts towards me and not evil, and because you know the plans you have for me, to give me a future and hope, you desire to see and make manifest that future and for us both to see it fulfilled.

As I walk through life, I walk in **CHRIST JESUS** and I can do <u>all</u> things in him who strengthens me. He said I shall do greater works than He did and I believe him! In the depths of my being I possess: The greater one in me, because *greater is He* who is <u>in me</u> than he who is in the world.

Father, I press toward the mark of the prize of the high calling of **GOD** and I always triumph in **CHRIST**. I will show forth your praise. Let the meditations of my heart and the words of my mouth be pleasing in your sight, oh **GOD!**

Father, as your son's blood *poured* out and your mercy *ran* to me. I became all your Word says that **I am.** Without you, I am nothing, because you are everything! As I think about you in my mind, it brings tears to my eyes. Everywhere you have taken me, it's been *by the hand* of Love. How could I ever say who I am, without saying who you are? Anything I have or am, it's because of you! You are the source of all my joy! You let nothing come to me that isn't for my growth and benefit to your Kingdom. Your Kingdom come, your will be done, on earth as it is in Heaven … Oh what a pleasure and honor it is to dine with **THE KING of KINGS**.

How can I ever say thank you?

With my life...

Here I am Lord,

Send Me ...

Your beloved,

Rebekah

Mrs. *Rebekah Lea Phelps*, full of **GOD'S** Glory, trusting in **JESUS**, being led by the **HOLY SPIRIT**...

The Author and Finisher of _my_ story!

Psalm of my Heart

*Who we are IN Christ**

Note from the Author:

This note "from the Author" could be a chapter in and of itself, but I think it's important for you to know just how it came about and some history behind it.

Prior to the writing this Psalm, I was spending a significant amount of time (over the span of 5 years, 1996 being the 5thth year) studying about:

- Who we are in Christ

- The Song of Solomon

- The Bride of Christ

- Our "rights" & authority as believers

It was absolutely the richest and the most intimate time in my walk with The Lord. It changed my heart & mind, the way I thought about *The Word,* the approach I had "with the enemy" in prayer, my belief system, the way I spoke or spoke up and much more. I had a huge "growth spurt", if you will, in those years. I pray this prayer helps launch you into a "new place" with your walk with the Lord.

At the time of writing this (February 7, 1996), I was living in Atlanta, GA. I'm not trying to sound like "a novel writer", but it was a bitterly cold winter's day with no sign of human life walking in the door (I was working in property management), and I had organized everything that could be organized and had nothing to do. So my mind went to "The Letter" I wanted to write to the Lord.

It had been on my heart for some time and all I knew was I wanted to write about who I AM in HIM. I never thought of it as a "Psalm" until sometime after it was done, and in reading it, it dawned on me that it was a "Psalm". Anytime the Lord mentioned it to me thereafter, He always referred to it as "The Psalm". I sat down that cold winter day at the typewriter and it literally flowed out of my heart, into my fingers and onto the keys. I remember the presence of the Lord, stopping to weep at times, and in 45 minutes or so, "It was finished." One thing I knew was that it was for me and to share with very few, if any...until he said, "it is time." So it got stuck in a binder & sat for years.

I'm sure if any of you have ever "waited on the Lord", his wait and our wait are two different things, but it's a great lesson on patience. I like to say it's *Yahweh*, not my way.

On March 4, 2015, I woke up about 9:00 am from a restless night. When I wake up in the middle of the night, I use this time to pray...so I did, almost all night. Upon awakening, I said, "Good Morning Lord" and I clearly heard the Lord say, "Publish the Psalm." You'd think I'd be jumping up and down saying, "Really Lord?! Now's the time?", but I didn't. I just smiled (yes, I was surprised), knew exactly what he meant and said, "Yes Sir." By the end of the day I had a contract signed with a publisher and then it dawned on me....

I had never looked up the scriptures that go with this "Psalm" until March 4, 2015, and the only reason I did was because the Lord brought a picture to my mind of a cross reference. I thought of putting this into an excel format so that those reading it would know this isn't just me talking, but the Holy Spirit using both the Old and New Testament in writing it. I'm amazed myself.

I've always said if I could tell a new believer (or an old one) to learn anything, it would be:

1. **Read the Gospels:** Matthew, Mark, Luke and John.

2. **PRAY and learn to give thanks IN ALL THINGS** (not **for**, but IN): Just PRAISE HIM and PRAISE HIM some more after you're done. It will be life changing. The primary

purpose of prayer should be praise, giving thanks and being grateful. God knows what you need better than you do; before it even rolls off the tongue he gave you, he knows what "orders" you're about to give him. He knows your wish list and what you think should happen, and He knows all the friends that told you what to pray for. You will find more "prayer" gets answered when you remember to praise him, and you worry less about tomorrow by doing so. Trust God, period. Try praying "if it be your will" or "on earth as it is in heaven" when you just can't help yourself "requesting" — you'll be surprised.

3. **Find out WHO YOU ARE ... IN HIM:** I don't think this is taught or even mentioned enough in churches. And yet to be effective IN PRAYER, as a witness, against Satan and as a light in the world, it's crucial you know WHO YOU ARE...IN HIM. Outside of HIM, you are nothing. IN HIM, you have nothing to worry about and Satan has everything to worry about. Now the shoe is on the other foot!

...And that's what the *Psalm of my Heart* is all about.

I'm speaking to you out of deep gratitude for all that God has given me, and especially as I have responsibilities in relation to you. Living then, as every one of you does, in pure grace, it's important that you not misinterpret yourselves as people who are bringing this goodness to God. No, God brings it all to you. The only accurate way to understand ourselves is by what God is and by what he does for us, not by what we are and what we do for him.

Roman 12:3 Message Bible

If you do not know Jesus Christ as your Savior:

I want you to have a prayer of salvation, but first there are a few things you should know: There is not an official prayer listed in scripture (it is implied) and it is found in Romans 10:9-10, "That if you confess with your mouth the Lord Jesus and believe in your heart that God has raised Him from the dead, you will be saved. For with the heart one believes unto righteousness, and with the mouth confession is made unto salvation." (NKJV) It is on my heart for you to read a prayer of salvation, so I have included one here.

Secondly, I want you to know that repentance means you are *turning to* God, and you are having *faith* and *trusting* that Christ will be true to HIS Word and forgive you. HE WILL meet you where you are. Remember: Grace doesn't give us an excuse to continue in our sin or harbor unforgiveness. True repentance brings change & the desire to "turn" from the old things and embrace the new. You are willfully laying down "your will" for HIS. You are accepting that Jesus Christ IS the Son of God. If you run into something difficult (like forgiving someone), ASK The Lord to help you, ask HIM to give you the desire to do so. Remember, no one has done anything to us that is worse than we have done to HIM (at the end of the day our sin is against HIM and HIM only). HE took OUR sin on himself!

Lastly, your walk doesn't "end" with a prayer (unless you're literally on your death bed), *it begins at this point*. I'm assigning "homework"... Now, find a good, solid, Biblically-based church and get a "foundation laid". Read the Gospels (Matthew, Mark, Luke and John) to learn who Jesus is and what he expects from you as his adopted son/daughter. Get baptized. It is an act of obedience and a public acknowledgment of HIM. Get a Bible if you don't have one. And above all, "be a doer" of what you learn.

You may not "feel" any different immediately (some do, some don't), but HE is at work in you, so take the "next steps of your journey". I look forward to meeting you in Heaven, if not before.

Welcome to the family of God, I'm rejoicing with Heaven …

Your sister in Christ,

PS: You may not know, but ALL of Heaven rejoices over one sinner coming to the Lord (Luke 15:10). Isn't that an amazing thought to ponder?

My *Father* in Heaven, I recognize you as *my* sovereign God, the creator of the universe and the creator of my heart. You knew me before I was even in my mother's womb.

I am coming to you, to acknowledge your son, *Jesus Christ*, as my Savior who came to die for my sins. Forgive me that it took me so long to humble myself and come to you. Forgive me of my selfish pride; forgive me of all my sins Father, known and unknown. I want your son to be my Lord and Savior, and welcome him to be my friend & teacher. I'm grateful you made Christ the way, the truth and the light rather than me having to live by law(s), by sacrifices and in eternal darkness away from you... I recognize, by faith, that HE became the sacrifice. Teach me your ways Lord; guide my feet to the straight and narrow path you laid out for me to take. Redeem the time I have lived without you Lord, and teach me how to use my life for your will and your purposes, until you return, no matter the cost. Put a watch over me Lord, and encompass me with strength when I am faced with my weaknesses. HELP me to flee temptations and see the way of escape that you will provide. Thank you Jesus for coming into my life and changing *me* to reflect *you*!

Amen. So be it and let it be so.

Now let HIM be the author and finisher of YOUR story!

To the Weary Believer:

Ecclesiastes 3 (NIV)

"A Time for Everything"

There is a time for everything, and a season for every activity under the heavens:

a time to be born and a time to die,

> a time to plant and a time to uproot,

a time to kill and **a time to heal,**

> a time to tear down and **a time to build,**

a time to weep and **a time to laugh,**

> a time to mourn and **a time to dance,**

a time to scatter stones and a time to gather them,

> a time to embrace and a time to refrain from embracing,

a time to search and **a time to give up,**

> a time to keep and a time to throw away,

a time to tear and **a time to mend,**

> **a time to be silent** and **a time to speak,**

a time to love and a time to hate,

> a time for war and **a time for peace."**

Greeting Brothers and Sisters *in Christ*,

I want to encourage you to "come home." But before you decide to read and pray, I want to say:

I have no idea why you are where you are, what all the stories and reasons are, who hurt you, abused you physically, mistook your kindness for weakness, or spiritually abused you, but I do know that no matter "who knows", the only one who can heal you is Christ and *He* knows all the details, even more than you ever knew or saw yourself. He holds your tears in a bottle; his hope is you'll surrender all your cares to HIM because he cares for you. It's time to allow him to restore your soul and heal your broken spirit.

My prayer for you is that you realize whatever happened is a reflection of man, NOT God. Those two people will never line up, not on this earth. No matter "how good" a person is, we are all vulnerable to sin and to hurting one another. I'm sorry you've encountered such trauma and tragedy or made choices that got you to this place of "dryness"; I know it's hard. I know it's difficult to trust again, to move out of fear and back into hope. It's a horrible feeling to feel like you've lost all hope, isn't it? Even to open your mouth and sing, or to go to church without sitting and crying takes effort. Or to open your Bible and "remember" what you were like (back then), but you can't see the pages because your eyes are full of tears... it's just too painful to simply read because you know you're too weary to walk.

My heart bleeds for those of you who have been battered without bruises, and my constant cry is, "Father, set the captives free – make a way of escape". If you're anything like most of us who have gone through abuse, you'd rather someone would have taken a bat to you rather than tear you down over time, destroy your identity "in Christ", damage, kill or take your children "just to get to you", and all sorts of other evils. Too many to mention here... but *Surrender.*

Just "come home" to HIM. Not to man, maybe not to the same fellowship or religion, but to HIS arms. Our walk with the Lord is NOT about "religion" but relationship! Close your eyes and "crawl up" in your daddy's lap where your healing is. Take baby steps. You know in your heart of hearts he'll meet you where you are. He isn't focused on your falls (any more than you would be as a parent watching a baby learn how to walk….again) but *your steps.*

Perhaps it's time to "tear down" those walls and go back to your foundation. Take time to weep and allow yourself to laugh. Take off the garments of mourning and grief and ask him to put HIS Joy back in you, and HIS robe of righteous over your shoulders. HE IS The Great Physician and HE WILL care for you in this healing time. He can take away your heart of stone and put in a heart of flesh; HE can replace mourning for joy. ASK HIM.

Your sister in Christ,

Rebekah Lea Phelps

PS: Keep in mind that at the end of the day, Christians aren't "perfect", just forgiven. Lastly, forgiveness doesn't always mean "restoration or relationship". One has nothing to do with the other. So just "forgive" and move on. One day, you'll stop gritting your teeth and "feel it."

Matthew 6:9-13 – "Our Father which art in heaven, Hallowed be thy name. Thy kingdom come, Thy will be done in earth, as it is in heaven. Give us this day our daily bread. And forgive us our debts, as we forgive our debtors. And lead us not into temptation*, but deliver us from evil: For thine is the kingdom, and the power, and the glory, forever. Amen."

Father, forgive me for being distant with you, for shutting you out, and for turning back to "Egypt" for my help, instead of to you who is my help in time of trouble. Forgive me for running away from you rather than running to you. I know you know... I am so (angry, hurt, afraid, mad, broken) that I have become "mute" and turned away from you. I have allowed myself to become "stale." I stopped being a doer of The Word. I feel like I've been serving on the front lines in battle and I'm weary. I allowed myself to get so weary that I just gave up and turned into my own emotions and reflections...I began to live by them instead of your Word. Forgive me Lord, my Father, my Friend, my Husband, my Healer and Counselor... *My Savior*. Hold me up with your right hand Lord, and teach me to walk again. I miss you, I love you. Forgive me Father.

Notes: * I pray "Do not allow me to be lead into temptation" but deliver me from evil. Reason is because the Word makes it known that Satan is the tempter NOT Christ. He is NOT "double minded"; his heart IS for you. The Word makes it clear that Satan petitions Christ to be allowed access to us, and NOTHING comes to us that HE hasn't allowed. Remember: God doesn't "discipline" those who he doesn't love, those who AREN'T his children.

Lastly, please let this prayer just be a guide for you and pray from YOUR heart. You know where you are and what applies to YOU. I hope you are encouraged just to begin again.

Scripture References:

Reference	Scripture	Verse (King James Version)	Paragraph
Abba Father, We cry	Rom 8:15	For ye have not received the spirit of bondage again to fear; but ye have received the Spirit of adoption, whereby we cry, Abba, Father.	6
Abide in Christ	John 15:5	I am the vine, ye are the branches: He that abideth in me, and I in him, the same bringeth forth much fruit: for without me ye can do nothing.	10
Abide under HIS shadow	Ps 91:1	He that dwelleth in the secret place of the most High shall abide under the shadow of the Almighty.	4
Abundant Grace	II Cor 4:15	For all things are for your sakes, that the abundant grace might through the thanksgiving of many redound to the glory of God.	2
Accepted in the beloved	Eph 1:6	To the praise of the glory of his grace, wherein he hath made us accepted in the beloved.	3
Access by one Spirit	Rom 5:2	For through him we both have access by one Spirit unto the Father.	7
Access to the Father	Eph 2:18	For through him we both have access by one Spirit unto the Father.	7

Reference	Scripture	Verse (King James Version)	Paragraph
Angels	Ps 91:11	For he shall give his angels charge over thee, to keep thee in all thy ways.	2
Angels	Luke 4:10	For it is written, He shall give his angels charge over thee, to keep thee.	2
Angels	Matt 18:10	Take heed that ye despise not one of these little ones; for I say unto you, That in heaven their angels do always behold the face of my Father which is in heaven.	2
Anoited me to...	Luke 4:18 - 19	"The Spirit of the Lord is upon me, because he has anointed me to proclaim good news to the poor. He has sent me to proclaim liberty to the captives and recovering of sight to the blind, to set at liberty those who are oppressed, To preach the acceptable year of the Lord.	5
Anointed to set captives free	Luke 4:18	"The Spirit of the Lord is upon me, because he has anointed me to proclaim good news to the poor. He has sent me to proclaim liberty to the captives and recovering of sight to the blind, to set at liberty those who are oppressed,	5

Reference	Scripture	Verse (King James Version)	Paragraph
Apostles & Prophets / Chief Cornerstone	Eph 2:20	And are built upon the foundation of the apostles and prophets, Jesus Christ himself being the chief corner stone;	4
Apple of his eye	Zech 2:8	For thus saith the LORD of hosts; After the glory hath he sent me unto the nations which spoiled you: for he that toucheth you toucheth the apple of his eye.	6
Apple of his eye	Deut 32:10	He found him in a desert land, and in the waste howling wilderness; he led him about, he instructed him, he kept him as the apple of his eye.	6
Apple of the eye	Ps 17:8	Keep me as the apple of the eye, hide me under the shadow of thy wings,	6
Authority over the enemy	Luke 10:19	Behold, I give unto you power to tread on serpents and scorpions, and over all the power of the enemy: and nothing shall by any means hurt you.	2
Before the womb he knew us	Jer 1:5	Before I formed thee in the belly I knew thee; and before thou camest forth out of the womb I sanctified thee, and I ordained thee a prophet unto the nations.	2

Reference	Scripture	Verse (King James Version)	Paragraph
Being Called	Rom 9:11	For the children being not yet born, neither having done any good or evil, that the purpose of God according to election might stand, not of works, but of him that calleth.	2
Beloved	I Thes 1:4	Knowing, brethren beloved, your election of God.	7
Beloved	I John 4:11	Beloved, if God so loved us, we ought also to love one another.	7
Beloved	I John 3:2	Beloved, now are we the sons of God, and it doth not yet appear what we shall be: but we know that, when he shall appear, we shall be like him; for we shall see him as he is.	7
Beloved, His	SOS 2:16	My beloved is mine, and I am his: he feedeth among the lilies.	10
Blame, In Love Elect	Eph 1:4	According as he hath chosen us in him before the foundation of the world, that we should be holy and without blame before him in love:	2
Blessed	Ps 118:26	Blessed be he that cometh in the name of the LORD: we have blessed you out of the house of the LORD.	2

Reference	Scripture	Verse (King James Version)	Paragraph
Blessed is the man	Ps 65:4	Blessed is the man whom thou choosest, and causest to approach unto thee, that he may dwell in thy courts: we shall be satisfied with the goodness of thy house, even of thy holy temple.	2
Blessed Us	Eph 1:3	Blessed be the God and Father of our Lord Jesus Christ, who hath blessed us with all spiritual blessings in heavenly places in Christ.	2
Blood poured out	Matt 26:28	For this is my blood of the new testament, which is shed for many for the remission of sins.	10
Blood shed / poured out	Luke 22:20	Likewise also the cup after supper, saying, This cup is the new testament in my blood, which is shed for you.	10
Body is the Temple	1 Cor 6:19	What? Know ye not that your body is the temple of the Holy Ghost which is in you, which ye have of God, and ye are not your own?	1
Born of God	1 John 5:4	For whatsoever is born of God overcometh the world: and this is the victory that overcometh the world, even our faith.	4

Reference	Scripture	Verse (King James Version)	Paragraph
Born of God	I John 5:18	We know that whosoever is born of God sinneth not; but he that is begotten of God keepeth himself, and that wicked one toucheth him not.	4
Bride of Christ	Eph 5:25-27	Husbands, love your wives, even as Christ also loved the church, and gave himself for it; that he might sanctify and cleanse it with the washing of water by the word, that he might present it to himself a glorious church, not having spot, or wrinkle, or any such thing; but that it should be holy and without blemish.	6
Call and the Lord will respond	Is 58:9	Then shalt thou call, and the LORD shall answer; thou shalt cry, and he shall say, Here I am. If thou take away from the midst of thee the yoke, the putting forth of the finger, and speaking vanity;	1
Called / Chosen	Matt 22:14	For many are called, but few are chosen.	6
Called by his grace	Gal 1:5	But when it pleased God, who separated me from my mother's womb, and called me by his grace,	2

Reference	Scripture	Verse (King James Version)	Paragraph
Called to be Saints	I Cor 1:2	Unto the church of God which is at Corinth, to them that are sanctified in Christ Jesus, called to be saints, with all that in every place call upon the name of Jesus Christ our Lord, both theirs and ours:	2
Cast out Devils	Mark 3:15	And to have power to heal sicknesses, and to cast out devils:	5
Chief of All Sinners	I Tim 1:15	This is a faithful saying, and worthy of all acceptation, that Christ Jesus came into the world to save sinners; of whom I am chief.	4
Chosen, God's	Deut 7:6	For thou art an holy people unto the LORD thy God: the LORD thy God hath chosen thee to be a special people unto himself, above all people that are upon the face of the earth.	3
Christ lives IN us	Gal 2:20	I am crucified with Christ: nevertheless I live; yet not I, but Christ liveth in me: and the life which I now live in the flesh I live by the faith of the Son of God, who loved me, and gave himself for me.	3

Reference	Scripture	Verse (King James Version)	Paragraph
Christ will complete his work in you	Phil 1:6	Being confident of this very thing, that he which hath begun a good work in you will perform it until the day of Jesus Christ:	3
Church of the Firstborn	Heb 12:23	To the general assembly and church of the first-born, which are written in heaven, and to God the Judge of all, and to the spirits of just men made perfect,	3
Cirsumcision	Eph 2:11	Wherefore remember, that ye being in time past Gentiles in the flesh, who are called uncircumcision by that which is called the circumcision in the flesh made by hand.	4
Complete in HIM	Col 2:10	And ye are complete in him, which is the head of all principality and power:	3
Condemnation, No	Rom 8:1	There is therefore now no condemnation to them which are in Christ Jesus, who walk not after the flesh, but after the Spirit.	7

Reference	Scripture	Verse (King James Version)	Paragraph
Condemned, Not	John 3:18	He that believeth on him is not condemned: but he that believeth not is condemned already, because he hath not believed in the name of the only begotten Son of God.	7
Conquerors	Rom 8:37	Nay, in all these things we are more than conquerors through him that loved us.	3
Conquerors	Rom 8:37	Nay, in all these things we are more than conquerors through him that loved us.	3
Consecrated (Separation)	II Cor 6: 17-18	Wherefore come out from among them, and be ye separate, saith the Lord, and touch not the unclean thing; and I will receive you, and will be a Father unto you, and ye shall be my sons and daughters, saith the Lord Almighty.	2
Continue in what you've learned	2 Tim 3:14	But continue thou in the things which thou hast learned and hast been assured of, knowing of whom thou hast learned them;	5

Reference	Scripture	Verse (King James Version)	Paragraph
Count my life as nothing	Acts 20:24	But none of these things move me, neither count I my life dear unto myself, so that I might finish my course with joy, and the ministry, which I have received of the Lord Jesus, to testify the gospel of the grace of God.	10
Cover us with a shield	Ps 5:12	For thou, LORD, wilt bless the righteous; with favour wilt thou compass him as with a shield.	4
Cover us with his feathers	Ps 91:4	He shall cover thee with his feathers, and under his wings shalt thou trust: his truth shall be thy shield and buckler.	4
Crush the serpant	Gen 3:15	And I will put enmity between thee and the woman, and between thy seed and her seed; it shall bruise thy head, and thou shalt bruise his heel.	2
Delivered from Darkness	Col 1:13	Who hath delivered us from the power of darkness, and hath translated us into the kingdom of his dear Son:	2

Reference	Scripture	Verse (King James Version)	Paragraph
Depth	Rom 8:30	Nor height, nor depth, nor any other creature, shall be able to separate us from the love of God, which is in Christ Jesus our Lord.	8
Devil walks the world, seeking	I Pet 5:8	Be sober, be vigilant; because your adversary the devil, as a roaring lion, walketh about, seeking whom he may devour:	8
Disciples follow him	Matt 16:24	Then said Jesus unto his disciples, If any man will come after me, let him deny himself, and take up his cross, and follow me.	5
Disciples, Continue in the Word	John 8:31	Then said Jesus to those Jews which believed on him, If ye continue in my word, then are ye my disciples indeed;	5
Doves eyes	SOS 1:15	Behold, thou art fair, my love; behold, thou art fair; thou hast doves' eyes.	6
Doves eyes	SOS 4:1	Behold, thou art fair, my love; behold, thou art fair; thou hast doves' eyes within thy locks: thy hair is as a flock of goats, that appear from mount Gilead.	6

Reference	Scripture	Verse (King James Version)	Paragraph
Draws us near	Jam 4:8	Draw nigh to God, and he will draw nigh to you. Cleanse your hands, ye sinners; and purify your hearts, ye double minded.	3
Draws us to himself	John 6:44	No man can come to me, except the Father which hath sent me draw him: and I will raise him up at the last day.	1
Earnest expectation	Rom 8:19	For the earnest expectation of the creature waiteth for the manifestation of the sons of God.	7
Earth as it is in heaven	Matt 6:10	Thy kingdom come. Thy will be done in earth, as it is in heaven.	10
Elect, The	Matt 24:22	And except those days should be shortened, there should no flesh be saved: but for the elect's sake those days shall be shortened.	3
Eternal Life / Salvation	I John 2:25	And this is the promise that he hath promised us, even eternal life.	7
Eternal Life / Salvation	Rom 6:23	For the wages of sin is death; but the gift of God is eternal life through Jesus Christ our Lord.	7

Reference	Scripture	Verse (King James Version)	Paragraph
Eternal Life / Salvation	Ps 139:23-24	Search me, O God, and know my heart: try me, and know my thoughts: And see if there be any wicked way in me, and lead me in the way everlasting.	7
Eternal Life / Salvation	I Pet 5:10	But the God of all grace, who hath called us unto his eternal glory by Christ Jesus, after that ye have suffered a while, make you perfect, stablish, strengthen, settle you.	7
Eternal Life / Salvation	John 3:16	For God so loved the world, that he gave his only begotten Son, that whosoever believeth in him should not perish, but have everlasting life.	7
Eternal Life / Salvation	I John 2:17	And the world passeth away, and the lust thereof: but he that doeth the will of God abideth for ever.	7
Eternal Life / Salvation	I John 5:13	These things have I written unto you that believe on the name of the Son of God; that ye may know that ye have eternal life, and that ye may believe on the name of the Son of God	7
Eternal Life / Salvation	II Cor 4:17	For our light affliction, which is but for a moment, worketh for us a far more exceeding and eternal weight of glory;	7

Reference	Scripture	Verse (King James Version)	Paragraph
Eternal Life / Salvation	Rom 8:18	For I reckon that the sufferings of this present time are not worthy to be compared with the glory which shall be revealed in us.	7
Eternal Life / Salvation	John 6:27	Labour not for the meat which perisheth, but for that meat which endureth unto everlasting life, which the Son of man shall give unto you: for him hath God the Father sealed.	7
Eternal Life / Salvation	Matt 7:13-14	Enter ye in at the strait gate: for wide is the gate, and broad is the way, that leadeth to destruction, and many there be which go in thereat: Because strait is the gate, and narrow is the way, which leadeth unto life, and few there be that find it.	7
Eternal Life / Salvation	John 4:14	But whosoever drinketh of the water that I shall give him shall never thirst; but the water that I shall give him shall be in him a well of water springing up into everlasting life.	7

Reference	Scripture	Verse (King James Version)	Paragraph
Eternal Life / Salvation	John 10:28-30	And I give unto them eternal life; and they shall never perish, neither shall any man pluck them out of my hand. My Father, which gave them me, is greater than all; and no man is able to pluck them out of my Father's hand. I and my Father are one.	7
Eternal Life / Salvation	Rev 1:8	I am Alpha and Omega, the beginning and the ending, saith the Lord, which is, and which was, and which is to come, the Almighty.	7
Eternal Life / Salvation	John 3:36	He that believeth on the Son hath everlasting life: and he that believeth not the Son shall not see life; but the wrath of God abideth on him.	7
Eternal Life / Salvation	John 17:3	And this is life eternal, that they might know thee the only true God, and Jesus Christ, whom thou hast sent.	7
Eternal Life / Salvation	I Tim 1:16	Howbeit for this cause I obtained mercy, that in me first Jesus Christ might shew forth all longsuffering, for a pattern to them which should hereafter believe on him to life everlasting.	7

Reference	Scripture	Verse (King James Version)	Paragraph
Eternal Life / Salvation	Ps 37:28	For the LORD loveth judgment, and forsaketh not his saints; they are preserved for ever: but the seed of the wicked shall be cut off.	7
Eternal Life / Salvation	Matt 10:39	He that findeth his life shall lose it: and he that loseth his life for my sake shall find it.	7
Eternal Life / Salvation	Gal 6:8	For he that soweth to his flesh shall of the flesh reap corruption; but he that soweth to the Spirit shall of the Spirit reap life everlasting.	7
Eternal Life / Salvation	Heb 7:25	Wherefore he is able also to save them to the uttermost that come unto God by him, seeing he ever liveth to make intercession for them.	7
Eternal Life / Salvation	Rom 5:21	That as sin hath reigned unto death, even so might grace reign through righteousness unto eternal life by Jesus Christ our Lord.	7
Evil can't touch us	I John 5:18	We know that whosoever is born of God sinneth not; but he that is begotten of God keepeth himself, and that wicked one toucheth him not.	4

Reference	Scripture	Verse (King James Version)	Paragraph
Eyes cry tears	Luke 23:28	But Jesus turning unto them said, Daughters of Jerusalem, weep not for me, but weep for yourselves, and for your children.	10
Eyes of Doves	SOS 5:12	His eyes are as the eyes of doves by the rivers of waters, washed with milk, and fitly set.	6
Father	Matt 23:9	And call no man your father upon the earth: for one is your Father, which is in heaven.	9
Favor (Grace) with God	Exo 34:9	And he said, If now I have found grace in thy sight, O Lord, let my Lord, I pray thee, go among us; for it is a stiffnecked people; and pardon our iniquity and our sin, and take us for thine inheritance.	5
Favor with Man	Esther 7:3	Then Esther the queen answered and said, If I have found favour in thy sight, O king, and if it please the king, let my life be given me at my petition, and my people at my request:	5
Fear, Spirit of	II Tim 1:7	For God hath not given us the spirit of fear; but of power, and of love, and of a sound mind.	6
Fellow citizen with the saints	Eph 2:19	Now therefore ye are no more strangers and foreigners, but fellowcitizens with the saints, and of the household of God;	4

Reference	Scripture	Verse (King James Version)	Paragraph
Fellow Citizens with the Saints	Eph 2:19	Now therefore ye are no more strangers and for-eigners, but fellowcitizens with the saints, and of the household of God;	2
Foot against a stone	Ps 91:12	They shall bear thee up in their hands, lest thou dash thy foot against a stone.	2
Free from Con-demnation	Rom 8:1	There is therefore now no condemnation to them which are in Christ Jesus, who walk not after the flesh, but after the Spirit.	3
Free of guilt	Rom 3:24	Being justified freely by his grace through the redemption that is in Christ Jesus:	7
Friends of the Lords	John 15:15	Henceforth I call you not servants; for the servant knoweth not what his lord doeth: but I have called you friends; for all things that I have heard of my Father I have made known unto you.	5
From Above	John 8:23	And he said unto them, Ye are from beneath; I am from above: ye are of this world; I am not of this world.	2
Gates in life	Matt 7:13	Enter ye in at the strait gate: for wide is the gate, and broad is the way, that leadeth to destruction, and many there be which go in thereat:	8

Reference	Scripture	Verse (King James Version)	Paragraph
Given us every-thing	2 Pe 1:3	According as his divine power hath given unto us all things that pertain unto life and godliness, through the knowledge of him that hath called us to glory and virtue:	10
Glory of the Lord	Is 60:1	Arise, shine; for thy light is come, and the glory of the LORD is risen upon thee.	7
Glory of the Lord	Is 60:1	Arise, shine; for thy light is come, and the glory of the LORD is risen upon thee.	10
Glory, God's	Is 6:3	And one cried unto another, and said, Holy, holy, holy, is the LORD of hosts: the whole earth is full of his glory.	10
God's thoughts towards us	Ps 139:17	How precious also are thy thoughts unto me, O God! how great is the sum of them!	7
Grace abounds	II Cor 9:8	And God is able to make all grace abound toward you; that ye, always having all sufficiency in all things, may abound to every good work:	2
Grace of God	I Cor 15: 10	But by the grace of God I am what I am: and his grace which was bestowed upon me was not in vain; but I laboured more abundantly than they all: yet not I, but the grace of God which was with me.	2

Reference	Scripture	Verse (King James Version)	Paragraph
Greater is He	I John 4:4	Ye are of God, little children, and have overcome them: because greater is he that is in you, than he that is in the world.	8
Greater works will we do	John 14:12	Verily, verily, I say unto you, He that believeth on me, the works that I do shall he do also; and greater works than these shall he do; because I go unto my Father.	7
Greater works, we will do	John 14:12	Verily, verily, I say unto you, He that believeth on me, the works that I do shall he do also; and greater works than these shall he do; because I go unto my Father.	8
Hands, His	John 3:35	The Father loveth the Son, and hath given all things into his hand.	10
Hands, His	John 20:20	And when he had so said, he shewed unto them his hands and his side. Then were the disciples glad, when they saw the Lord.	10
He is our strenght & joy	Ps 28:7	The LORD is my strength and my shield; my heart trusted in him, and I am helped: therefore my heart greatly rejoiceth; and with my song will I praise him.	1

Reference	Scripture	Verse (King James Version)	Paragraph
Head not the Tail	Deut 28:13	And the LORD shall make thee the head, and not the tail; and thou shalt be above only, and thou shalt not be beneath; if that thou hearken unto the commandments of the LORD thy God, which I command thee this day, to observe and to do them:	2
Heal the broken hearted	Luke 4:18	"The Spirit of the Lord is upon me, because he has anointed me to proclaim good news to the poor. He has sent me to proclaim liberty to the captives and recovering of sight to the blind, to set at liberty those who are oppressed..."	5
Heal the sick, raise the dead...	Matt 10:8	Heal the sick, cleanse the lepers, raise the dead, cast out devils: freely ye have received, freely give.	5
Healed, by his stripes	I Pet 2:24	Who his own self bare our sins in his own body on the tree, that we, being dead to sins, should live unto righteousness: by whose stripes ye were healed.	7
Healed, by his wounds	Is 53:5	But he was wounded for our transgressions, he was bruised for our iniquities: the chastisement of our peace was upon him; and with his stripes we are healed.	7

Reference	Scripture	Verse (King James Version)	Paragraph
Heart of Stone to a heart of flesh	Eze 36:26	A new heart also will I give you, and a new spirit will I put within you: and I will take away the stony heart out of your flesh, and I will give you an heart of flesh.	1
Hearts to fullfill his will	Rev 17:17	For God hath put in their hearts to fulfil his will, and to agree, and give their kingdom unto the beast, until the words of God shall be fulfilled.	7
Heirs	Rom 8:17	And if children, then heirs; heirs of God, and joint-heirs with Christ; if so be that we suffer with him, that we may be also glorified together.	3
Here I am Lord, Send me	Is 6:8	Also I heard the voice of the Lord, saying, Whom shall I send, and who will go for us? Then said I, Here am I; send me.	10
Hiden in Christ	Col 3:1-4	If ye then be risen with Christ, seek those things which are above, where Christ sitteth on the right hand of God. Set your affection on things above, not on things on the earth. For ye are dead, and your life is hid with Christ in God. When Christ, who is our life, shall appear, then shall ye also appear with him in glory.	7

Reference	Scripture	Verse (King James Version)	Paragraph
High Calling	Phil 3:14	I press toward the mark for the prize of the high calling of God in Christ Jesus.	9
Holiness	I Pet 1:16	Because it is written, Be ye holy; for I am holy.	2
Holy	Lev 11:44	For I am the LORD your God: ye shall therefore sanctify your-selves, and ye shall be holy; for I am holy: nei-ther shall ye defile yourselves with any manner of creeping thing that creepeth upon the earth.	2
Holy Ghose dwells in us	II Tim 1:14	That good thing which was committed unto thee keep by the Holy Ghost which dwelleth in us.	1
Home, Earth is not our home	Heb 13:14	For here have we no continuing city, but we seek one to come. (Also see other versions that reference "home")	6
Home, in the body, absent from the Lord	II Cor 5:6	Therefore we are always confident, knowing that, whilst we are at home in the body, we are absent from the Lord:	6
Husband, Maker is	Is 54:5	For thy Maker is thine husband; the LORD of hosts is his name; and thy Redeemer the Holy One of Israel; The God of the whole earth shall he be called.	6

Reference	Scripture	Verse (King James Version)	Paragraph
Image, changed into his	II Cor 3:18	But we all, with open face beholding as in a glass the glory of the Lord, are changed into the same image from glory to glory, even as by the Spirit of the Lord.	7
Inheritance	Col 1:12	Giving thanks unto the Father, which hath made us meet to be partakers of the inheritance of the saints in light.	3
Incorruptible seed	I Peter 1:23	Being born again, not of corruptible seed, but of incorruptible, by the word of God, which liveth and abideth for ever.	1
Intercession against principalities, powers and rulers of darkness	Eph 6:12	For we wrestle not against flesh and blood, but against principalities, against powers, against the rulers of the darkness of this world, against spiritual wickedness in high places.	5
Intercession, Christ	Rom 8:34	Who is he that condemneth? It is Christ that died, yea rather, that is risen again, who is even at the right hand of God, who also maketh intercession for us.	5

Reference	Scripture	Verse (King James Version)	Paragraph
Intercession, Come bodly to the throne	Heb 4:16	Let us therefore come boldly unto the throne of grace, that we may obtain mercy, and find grace to help in time of need.	5
Intercession, Jesus intercedes for us at the right hand of God	Rom 8:34	Who is he that condemneth? It is Christ that died, yea rather, that is risen again, who is even at the right hand of God, who also maketh intercession for us.	5
Joy of the Lord is our strenght	Neh 8:10	Then he said unto them, Go your way, eat the fat, and drink the sweet, and send portions unto them for whom nothing is prepared: for this day is holy unto our Lord: neither be ye sorry; for the joy of the LORD is your strength.	1
Joy, Exceeding	Ps 43:4	Then will I go unto the altar of God, unto God my exceeding joy: yea, upon the harp will I praise thee, O God my God.	10
King of Kings	Rev 19:16	And he hath on his vesture and on his thigh a name written, KING OF KINGS, AND LORD OF LORDS.	10
Kingdom come	Matt 6:10	Thy kingdom come. Thy will be done in earth, as it is in heaven.	10

Reference	Scripture	Verse (King James Version)	Paragraph
Kings, before	Prov 22:9	Seest thou a man diligent in his business? he shall stand before kings; he shall not stand before mean men.	10
Lay down our lives	John 15:13	Greater love hath no man than this, that a man lay down his life for his friends.	7
Lay down our lives	I John 3:16	Hereby perceive we the love of God, because he laid down his life for us: and we ought to lay down our lives for the brethren.	7
Lay hands on the sick	Mark 16:17-18	And these signs shall follow them that believe; In my name shall they cast out devils; they shall speak with new tongues; They shall take up serpents; and if they drink any deadly thing, it shall not hurt them; they shall lay hands on the sick, and they shall recover.	5
Leads us besides still waters	Ps 23:2	He maketh me to lie down in green pastures: he leadeth me beside the still waters.	5
Life and favour, Granted	Job 10:12	Thou hast granted me life and favour, and thy visitation hath preserved my spirit.	5
Light of the world	Matt 5:14	Ye are the light of the world. A city that is set on an hill cannot be hid.	6

Reference	Scripture	Verse (King James Version)	Paragraph
Living epistle	II Cor 3:2	Ye are our epistle written in our hearts, known and read of all men:	6
Lord is our shepherd	Ps 23:1	The LORD is my shepherd; I shall not want.	5
Lord of Host is his name	Is 54:5	For thy Maker is thine husband; the LORD of hosts is his name; and thy Redeemer the Holy One of Israel; The God of the whole earth shall he be called.	6
Lord's thoughts of peace to us, not evil	Jer 29:11	For I know the thoughts that I think toward you, saith the LORD, thoughts of peace, and not of evil, to give you an expected end.	7
Love	I Cor 13:1-13	Though I speak with the tongues of men and of angels, and have not charity, I am become as sounding brass, or a tinkling cymbal. And though I have the gift of prophecy, and understand all mysteries, and all knowledge; and though I have all faith, so that I could remove mountains, and have not charity, I am nothing. And though I bestow all my goods to feed the poor, and though I give my body to be burned, and have not charity, it profiteth me nothing. Charity suffereth long, and is kind;	6

Reference	Scripture	Verse (King James Version)	Paragraph
Love (continued)	I Cor 13:1-13	charity envieth not; charity vaunteth not itself, is not puffed up, doth not behave itself unseemly, seeketh not her own, is not easily provoked, thinketh no evil; rejoiceth not in iniquity, but rejoiceth in the truth; beareth all things, believeth all things, hopeth all things, endureth all things. Charity never faileth: but whether there be prophecies, they shall fail; whether there be tongues, they shall cease; whether there be knowledge, it shall vanish away. For we know in part, and we prophesy in part. But when that which is perfect is come, then that which is in part shall be done away. When I was a child, I spake as a child, I understood as a child, I thought as a child: but when I became a man, I put away childish things. For now we see through a glass, darkly; but then face to face: now I know in part; but then shall I know even as also I am known. And now abideth faith, hope, charity, these three; but the greatest of these is charity.	6

Reference	Scripture	Verse (King James Version)	Paragraph
Marriage of the Lamb	Rev 19:7-9	Let us be glad and rejoice, and give honour to him: for the marriage of the Lamb is come, and his wife hath made herself ready. And to her was granted that she should be arrayed in fine linen, clean and white: for the fine linen is the righteousness of saints. And he saith unto me, Write, Blessed are they which are called unto the marriage supper of the Lamb. And he saith unto me, These are the true sayings of God.	6
Marvelous light	I Pet 2:9	But ye are a chosen generation, a royal priesthood, an holy nation, a peculiar people; that ye should shew forth the praises of him who hath called you out of darkness into his marvellous light:	2
Meditations of my Heart	Ps 19:14	Let the words of my mouth, and the meditation of my heart, be acceptable in thy sight, O LORD, my strength, and my redeemer.	9
Mercy	James 2:13	For he shall have judgment without mercy, that hath shewed no mercy; and mercy rejoiceth against judgment.	10

Reference	Scripture	Verse (King James Version)	Paragraph
Mercy	Mic 6:8	He hath shewed thee, O man, what is good; and what doth the LORD require of thee, but to do justly, and to love mercy, and to walk humbly with thy God?	10
Mercy	2 Pet 3:9	The Lord is not slack concerning his promise, as some men count slackness; but is long-suffering to us-ward, not willing that any should perish, but that all should come to repentance.	10
Mercy vs. Sacrifice	Matt 9:13	But go ye and learn what that meaneth, I will have mercy, and not sacrifice: for I am not come to call the righteous, but sinners to repentance.	10
Mind of Christ	1 Cor 2:16	For who hath known the mind of the Lord, that he may instruct him? But we have the mind of Christ.	4
Morning into Dancing	Ps 30:11	Thou hast turned for me my mourning into dancing: thou hast put off my sackcloth, and girded me with gladness;	3
New Creature	Gal 6:15	For in Christ Jesus neither circumcision availeth any thing, nor uncircumcision, but a new creature.	1

Reference	Scripture	Verse (King James Version)	Paragraph
New Creature, In Christ	II Cor 5:17	Therefore if any man be in Christ, he is a new creature: old things are passed away; behold, all things are become new.	1
Nothing shall hurt you	Luke 10:19	Behold, I give unto you power to tread on serpents and scorpions, and over all the power of the enemy: and nothing shall by any means hurt you.	5
Nothing without Him	John 15:5	I am the vine, ye are the branches: He that abideth in me, and I in him, the same bringeth forth much fruit: for without me ye can do nothing.	10
Old Man crucified with Christ	Rom 6:6	Knowing this, that our old man is crucified with him, that the body of sin might be destroyed, that henceforth we should not serve sin.	3
Overcome the World	I John 5:4-5	For whatsoever is born of God overcometh the world: and this is the victory that overcometh the world, even our faith. Who is he that overcometh the world, but he that believeth that Jesus is the Son of God?	7

Reference	Scripture	Verse (King James Version)	Paragraph
Overcome, because He did	John 16:33	These things I have spoken unto you, that in me ye might have peace. In the world ye shall have tribulation: but be of good cheer; I have overcome the world.	1
Parable of the Dinner	Luke 14:15-24	When one of those who were reclining at the table with Him heard this, he said to Him, "Blessed is everyone who will eat bread in the kingdom of God!" But He said to him, "A man was giving a big dinner, and he invited many; and at the dinner hour he sent his slave to say to those who had been invited, 'Come; for everything is ready now.' "But they all alike began to make excuses. The first one said to him, 'I have bought a piece of land and I need to go out and look at it; please consider me excused.' "Another one said, 'I have bought five yoke of oxen, and I am going to try them out; please consider me excused.' "Another one said, 'I have married a wife, and for that reason I cannot come.' "And the slave came back and reported this to his master.	10

Reference	Scripture	Verse (King James Version)	Paragraph
Parable of the Dinner (continued)	Luke 14:15-24	Then the head of the household became angry and said to his slave, 'Go out at once into the streets and lanes of the city and bring in here the poor and crippled and blind and lame.' "And the slave said, 'Master, what you commanded has been done, and still there is room.' "And the master said to the slave, 'Go out into the highways and along the hedges, and compel them to come in, so that my house may be filled. 'For I tell you, none of those men who were invited shall taste of my dinner.'"	10
Partaker of HIS divine nature	II Peter 1:4	Whereby are given unto us exceeding great and precious promises: that by these ye might be partakers of the divine nature, having escaped the corruption that is in the world through lust.	4
Peace of God	Phil 4:7	And the peace of God, which passeth all understanding, shall keep your hearts and minds through Christ Jesus.	7
Plague	Ps 91:10	There shall no evil befall thee, neither shall any plague come nigh thy dwelling.	7

Reference	Scripture	Verse (King James Version)	Paragraph
Plans he has for us	Jer 29:11	For I know the thoughts that I think toward you, saith the LORD, thoughts of peace, and not of evil, to give you an expected end.	7
Power of the Holy Ghost	Acts 1:8	But ye shall receive power, after that the Holy Ghost is come upon you: and ye shall be witnesses unto me both in Jerusalem, and in all Judaea, and in Samaria, and unto the uttermost part of the earth.	5
Power over ALL the power of the enemy	Luke 10:19	Behold, I give unto you power to tread on serpents and scorpions, and over all the power of the enemy: and nothing shall by any means hurt you.	5
Power to heal	Mark 3:15	And to have power to heal sicknesses, and to cast out devils:	5
Predestined to be conformed	Rom 8:29	For whom he did foreknow, he also did predestinate to be conformed to the image of his Son, that he might be the firstborn among many brethren.	3
Press towards the mark	Phil 3:14	I press toward the mark for the prize of the high calling of God in Christ Jesus.	9

Reference	Scripture	Verse (King James Version)	Paragraph
Prosperous, what your hand touches	Deut 30:9	And the LORD thy God will make thee plenteous in every work of thine hand, in the fruit of thy body, and in the fruit of thy cattle, and in the fruit of thy land, for good: for the LORD will again rejoice over thee for good, as he rejoiced over thy fathers:	5
Raised up	Rom 8:11	But if the Spirit of him that raised up Jesus from the dead dwell in you, he that raised up Christ from the dead shall also quicken your mortal bodies by his Spirit that dwelleth in you.	7
Raised up with Christ	Eph 2:6	And hath raised us up together, and made us sit together in heavenly places in Christ Jesus:	7
Raised up with Christ	Col 3:1	If ye then be risen with Christ, seek those things which are above, where Christ sitteth on the right hand of God.	7
Reconcilled to God	II Cor 5:8	And all things are of God, who hath reconciled us to himself by Jesus Christ, and hath given to us the ministry of reconciliation;	3

Reference	Scripture	Verse (King James Version)	Paragraph
Redeemed from the curse of the law	Gal 3:13	Christ hath redeemed us from the curse of the law, being made a curse for us: for it is written, Cursed is every one that hangeth on a tree:	2
Refuge and fortress	Ps 91:2	I will say of the LORD, He is my refuge and my fortress: my God; in him will I trust.	4
Respresentatives of Christ	II Cor 5:20	Now then we are ambassadors for Christ, as though God did beseech you by us: we pray you in Christ's stead, be ye reconciled to God.	6
Restoration of your soul	Ps 23:3	He restoreth my soul: he leadeth me in the paths of righteousness for his name's sake.	4
Restores my soul	Ps 23:3	He restoreth my soul: he leadeth me in the paths of righteousness for his name's sake.	5
Rich not poor	II Cor 8:9	For ye know the grace of our Lord Jesus Christ, that, though he was rich, yet for your sakes he became poor, that ye through his poverty might be rich.	3

Reference	Scripture	Verse (King James Version)	Paragraph
Righteousness	Rom 5:18-19	Therefore as by the offence of one judgment came upon all men to condemnation; even so by the righteousness of one the free gift came upon all men unto justification of life. For as by one man's disobedience many were made sinners, so by the obedience of one shall many be made righteous.	2
Righteousness of God, IN Christ Jesus	II Cor 5:21	For he hath made him to be sin for us, who knew no sin; that we might be made the righteousness of God in him.	4
Righteousness, be made	II Cor 5:21	For he hath made him to be sin for us, who knew no sin; that we might be made the righteousness of God in him.	10
Rooted & Built up in Him	Col 2:6-7	As ye have therefore received Christ Jesus the Lord, so walk ye in him: Rooted and built up in him, and stablished in the faith, as ye have been taught, abounding therein with thanksgiving.	4
Saints in Light	Col 1:12	Giving thanks unto the Father, which hath made us meet to be partakers of the inheritance of the saints in light:	2

Reference	Scripture	Verse (King James Version)	Paragraph
Saints in the Earth	Ps 16:3	But to the saints that are in the earth, and to the excellent, in whom is all my delight.	2
Salt of the earth	Matt 5:13	Ye are the salt of the earth: but if the salt have lost his savour, wherewith shall it be salted? it is thenceforth good for nothing, but to be cast out, and to be trodden under foot of men.	6
Sanctified, Justified	I Cor 6:11	And such were some of you: but ye are washed, but ye are sanctified, but ye are justified in the name of the Lord Jesus, and by the Spirit of our God.	2
Sanctify (Consecrate)	Joshua 3:5	And Joshua said unto the people, Sanctify yourselves: for to morrow the LORD will do wonders among you.	2
Sealed by God	II Cor 1:22	Who hath also sealed us, and given the earnest of the Spirit in our hearts.	7
Sealed Us	II Cor 1:22	Who hath also sealed us, and given the earnest of the Spirit in our hearts.	3

Reference	Scripture	Verse (King James Version)	Paragraph
Seated in Heavenly Places	Eph 2: 4-7	But God, who is rich in mercy, for his great love wherewith he loved us Even when we were dead in sins, hath quickened us together with Christ, (by grace ye are saved;) And hath raised us up together, and made us sit together in heavenly places in Christ Jesus: That in the ages to come he might shew the exceeding riches of his grace in his kindness toward us through Christ Jesus.	7
Seek to Save = lose	Matt 16:25	For whosoever will save his life shall lose it: and whosoever will lose his life for my sake shall find it.	7
Set Apart	Ps 4:3	But know that the LORD hath set apart him that is godly for himself: the LORD will hear when I call unto him.	2
Set Free	John 8:36	If the Son therefore shall make you free, ye shall be free indeed.	3
Set free & made strong in weakiness	II Cor 12:9-10	And he said unto me, My grace is sufficient for thee: for my strength is made perfect in weakness. Most gladly therefore will I rather glory in my infirmities, that the power of Christ may rest upon me. for Christ's sake: for when I am weak, then am I strong.	3

Reference	Scripture	Verse (King James Version)	Paragraph
Shame of your youth taken	Is 54:4	Fear not; for thou shalt not be ashamed: neither be thou confounded; for thou shalt not be put to shame: for thou shalt forget the shame of thy youth, and shalt not remember the reproach of thy widow-hood any more.	7
Shew forth Praise	I Peter 2:9	But ye are a chosen generation, a royal priesthood, an holy nation, a peculiar peo-ple; that ye should shew forth the praises of him who hath called you out of darkness into his marvellous light:	9
Sign shall follow them who believe, These	Mark 16:17-18	And these signs shall follow them that believe; In my name shall they cast out dev-ils; they shall speak with new tongues; They shall take up serpents; and if they drink any deadly thing, it shall not hurt them; they shall lay hands on the sick, and they shall recover.	5
Sitting with a ruler	Prov 23:1	When thou sittest to eat with a ruler, con-sider diligently what is before thee:	10

Reference	Scripture	Verse (King James Version)	Paragraph
Sorrow turned to Joy	John 16:20	Verily, verily, I say unto you, That ye shall weep and lament, but the world shall rejoice: and ye shall be sorrowful, but your sorrow shall be turned into joy.	3
Sound Mind	II Timothy 1:7	For God hath not given us the spirit of fear; but of power, and of love, and of a sound mind.	6
Spirit, His, in our hearts	II Cor 1:22	Who hath also sealed us, and given the earnest of the Spirit in our hearts.	7
Sprit of Jesus resides in us, Abba Father	Gal 4:6	And because ye are sons, God hath sent forth the Spirit of his Son into your hearts, crying, Abba, Father.	6
Strenght and Weakness	II Cor 12:9	And he said unto me, My grace is sufficient for thee: for my strength is made perfect in weakness. Most gladly therefore will I rather glory in my infirmities, that the power of Christ may rest upon me.	3
Submit, resist & devil must flee	James 4:7	Submit yourselves therefore to God. Resist the devil, and he will flee from you.	7

Reference	Scripture	Verse (King James Version)	Paragraph
Teacher come from God	John 3:2	The same came to Jesus by night, and said unto him, Rabbi, we know that thou art a teacher come from God: for no man can do these miracles that thou doest, except God be with him.	5
Teacher with compassion for unlearned	Mark 6:34	And Jesus, when he came out, saw much people, and was moved with compassion toward them, because they were as sheep not having a shepherd: and he began to teach them many things.	5
Teacher, Christ is our Teacher	Matt 23:10	Neither be ye called masters: for one is your Master, even Christ.	5
Temptation	I Cor 10:13	There hath no temptation taken you but such as is common to man: but God is faithful, who will not suffer you to be tempted above that ye are able; but will with the temptation also make a way to escape, that ye may be able to bear it.	10

Reference	Scripture	Verse (King James Version)	Paragraph
Thank God with your own life	Rom 12:1-21	I beseech you therefore, brethren, by the mercies of God, that ye present your bodies a living sacrifice, holy, acceptable unto God, which is your reasonable service. And be not conformed to this world: but be ye transformed by the renewing of your mind, that ye may prove what is that good, and acceptable, and perfect, will of God. For I say, through the grace given unto me, to every man that is among you, not to think of himself more highly than he ought to think; but to think soberly, according as God hath dealt to every man the measure of faith. For as we have many members in one body, and all members have not the same office: So we, being many, are one body in Christ, and every one members one of another. Having then gifts differing according to the grace that is given to us, whether prophecy, let us prophesy according to the proportion of faith; Or ministry, let us wait on our ministering: or he that teacheth, on teaching; Or he that exhorteth, on exhortation: he that	10

Reference	Scripture	Verse (King James Version)	Paragraph
Thank God with your own life (continued)	Rom 12:1-21	giveth, let him do it with simplicity; he that ruleth, with diligence; he that sheweth mercy, with cheerfulness. Let love be without dis-simulation. Abhor that which is evil; cleave to that which is good. Be kindly affectioned one to another with broth-erly love; in honour preferring one another; Not slothful in busi-ness; fervent in spirit; serving the Lord; Rejoicing in hope; patient in tribulation; continuing instant in prayer; Distributing to the necessity of saints; given to hospitality. Bless them which per-secute you: bless, and curse not. Rejoice with them that do rejoice, and weep with them that weep. Be of the same mind one toward another. Mind not high things, but condescend to men of low estate. Be not wise in your own conceits. Recom-pense to no man evil for evil. Provide things honest in the sight of all men. If it be possible, as much as lieth in you, live peaceably with all men. Dearly beloved,	10

Reference	Scripture	Verse (King James Version)	Paragraph
Thank God with your own life (continued)	Rom 12:1-21	avenge not yourselves, but rather give place unto wrath: for it is written, Vengeance is mine; I will repay, saith the Lord. Therefore if thine enemy hunger, feed him; if he thirst, give him drink: for in so doing thou shalt heap coals of fire on his head. Be not overcome of evil, but overcome evil with good.	10
Thanking God	I Thes 3:9-13	For what thanks can we render to God again for you, for all the joy wherewith we joy for your sakes before our God; Night and day praying exceedingly that we might see your face, and might perfect that which is lacking in your faith? Now God himself and our Father, and our Lord Jesus Christ, direct our way unto you. And the Lord make you to increase and abound in love one toward another, and toward all men, even as we do toward you: To the end he may stablish your hearts unblame-able in holiness before God, even our Father, at the coming of our Lord Jesus Christ with all his saints.	10

Reference	Scripture	Verse (King James Version)	Paragraph
Time for Everything	Ecc 3:1-8	To every thing there is a season, and a time to every purpose under the heaven: A time to be born, and a time to die; a time to plant, and a time to pluck up that which is planted; A time to kill, and a time to heal; a time to break down, and a time to build up; A time to weep, and a time to laugh; a time to mourn, and a time to dance; A time to cast away stones, and a time to gather stones together; a time to embrace, and a time to refrain from embracing; A time to get, and a time to lose; a time to keep, and a time to cast away; A time to rend, and a time to sew; a time to keep silence, and a time to speak; A time to love, and a time to hate; a time of war, and a time of peace.	5
To the end ye may be established;	Rom 1:11	For I long to see you, that I may impart unto you some spiritual gift, to the end ye may be established.	2

Reference	Scripture	Verse (King James Version)	Paragraph
Triumph in Christ	II Cor 2:14	Now thanks be unto God, which always causeth us to triumph in Christ, and maketh manifest the savour of his knowledge by us in every place.	9
Under our feet	Rom 16:20	And the God of peace shall bruise Satan under your feet shortly. The grace of our Lord Jesus Christ be with you. Amen.	2
Value others beyond self	Phil 2:3	Let nothing be done through strife or vain-glory; but in lowliness of mind let each esteem other better than themselves.	10
Victory through Christ	I Cor 15:57	But thanks be to God, which giveth us the victory through our Lord Jesus Christ.	3
Victourious by the blood of the lamb	Rev 12:11	And they overcame him by the blood of the Lamb, and by the word of their testi-mony; and they loved not their lives unto the death.	3
Virgin to Christ, Bride	II Cor 11:2	For I am jealous over you with godly jealousy: for I have espoused you to one husband, that I may present you as a chaste virgin to Christ.	6

Reference	Scripture	Verse (King James Version)	Paragraph
Wait on the Lord	Is 40:31	But they that wait upon the LORD shall renew their strength; they shall mount up with wings as eagles; they shall run, and not be weary; and they shall walk, and not faint.	4
Walk in the light	I John 1:6-7	If we say that we have fellowship with him, and walk in darkness, we lie, and do not the truth: But if we walk in the light, as he is in the light, we have fellowship one with another, and the blood of Jesus Christ his Son cleanseth us from all sin.	8
Walking through this life	II Cor 5:7	(For we walk by faith, not by sight:)	8
Washed in the blood of the lamb	Rev 7:14	And I said unto him, Sir, thou knowest. And he said to me, These are they which came out of great tribulation, and have washed their robes, and made them white in the blood of the Lamb.	1
Ways & Thoughts	Is 55:8-9	For my thoughts are not your thoughts, neither are your ways my ways, saith the LORD. For as the heavens are higher than the earth, so are my ways higher than your ways, and my thoughts than your thoughts.	10

Reference	Scripture	Verse (King James Version)	Paragraph
We can do all things IN Him	Phil 4:13	I can do all things through Christ which strengtheneth me.	8
Weapon, None shall prosper	Is 54:17	No weapon that is formed against thee shall prosper; and every tongue that shall rise against thee in judgment thou shalt condemn. This is the heritage of the servants of the LORD, and their righteousness is of me, saith the LORD.	7
Weep not for Jesus	Luke 23:28	But Jesus turning unto them said, Daughters of Jerusalem, weep not for me, but weep for yourselves, and for your children.	10
Who is against us? Justifies us, Intercedes for us, Nothing will separate us from HIM,	Rom 8:31-39	What then shall we say to these things? If God is for us, who is against us? He who did not spare His own Son, but delivered Him over for us all, how will He not also with Him freely give us all things? Who will bring a charge against God's elect? God is the one who justifies; who is the one who condemns? Christ Jesus is He who died, yes, rather who was raised, who is at the right hand of God, who also intercedes for us.	3

Reference	Scripture	Verse (King James Version)	Paragraph
Who is against us? Justifies us, Intercedes for us, Nothing will separate us from HIM, (continued)	Rom 8:31-39	Who will separate us from the love of Christ? Will tribulation, or distress, or persecution, or famine, or nakedness, or peril, or sword? Just as it is written, "FOR YOUR SAKE WE ARE BEING PUT TO DEATH ALL DAY LONG; WE WERE CONSIDERED AS SHEEP TO BE SLAUGHTERED." But in all these things we overwhelmingly conquer through Him who loved us. For I am convinced that neither death, nor life, nor angels, nor principalities, nor things present, nor things to come, nor powers, nor height, nor depth, nor any other created thing, will be able to separate us from the love of God, which is in Christ Jesus our Lord.	3

Reference	Scripture	Verse (King James Version)	Paragraph
Wings as Eagles	Is 40:31	But they that wait upon the LORD shall renew their strength; they shall mount up with wings as eagles; they shall run, and not be weary; and they shall walk, and not faint.	4
Wisdom, Ask	James 1:5-6	If any of you lack wisdom, let him ask of God, that giveth to all men liberally, and upbraideth not; and it shall be given him. But let him ask in faith, nothing wavering. For he that wavereth is like a wave of the sea driven with the wind and tossed.	10
Words of my Mouth	Ps 19:14	Let the words of my mouth, and the meditation of my heart, be acceptable in thy sight, O LORD, my strength, and my redeemer.	9

Rebekah Lea Phelps

Rebekah is also the author of *"I'm an Eagle, Not A Field Chick"*, which is an allegory about an eagle's egg that falls from a nest, lands on the back of a dove (representing God) and hatches in a hens nest (signifying parental oversight). The eaglet, later to be known as Goldie, is raised on a farm (indicating a diverse suburb) and must discover who she was created to be and who she really is!

Rebekah is an entrepreneur and artist. She founded *Extra You LLC* and *White House Home Inventory*. Her businesses have served the D.C. metro area since 2005. She is happily married to George Phelps and together they have a Maine Coon cat they wait on, named Tipper Puppy. They now reside in West Virginia and attend Cornerstone Chapel in Leesburg, Virginia.

Rebekah would love to hear from you and can be reached at her author website www.RebekahLeaPhelps.com or www.ExtraYou.net

The Author, *Rebekah,* would love to have your feedback and hear from you.

She has designed a piece of stationary on the following page, for you to tear from the book and mail.

Please don't forget to print clearly your name, address and email so she can respond to you and add you to her mailing list.

Psalm
of my
Heart

Who We Are In Christ

Please PRINT Your Name:
Please PRINT Your Email:

I am the vine, ye are the branches:
He that abideth in me, and I in him, the same bringeth forth
much fruit: for without me ye can do nothing.
-John 15:5

Rebekah Lea Phelps
P.O. Box 235
Charles Town WV 25414

Illustrations by Aaron Hover ~ www.mountainofstrength.net

"Psalm of my Heart" and "I'm an Eagle Not a Field Chick"

www.RebekahLeaPhelps.com

CPSIA information can be obtained
at www.ICGtesting.com
Printed in the USA
LVOW01s1056131115

462330LV00016BA/70/P